British Library Cataloguing in Publication Data

Testa, Fulvio
  If you take a pencil.
  1. Numeration—Pictorial works—Juvenile literature
  I. Title
  513'.5 QA141.3

  ISBN 0-86264-032-6

If You Take a Pencil
FULVIO TESTA

Andersen Press · London

Hutchinson of Australia

If you take a pencil, you can draw two cats.

And if they like each other, there will soon be three.

They will flirt with four birds in a golden cage.

And five fingers can give them freedom.

They will fly into a garden with six orange trees.

Nearby is a fountain with seven jets of fresh water.

In the fountain are eight red fish with blue tails—

blue like the sea where there is a boat with nine sails.

Ten are the sailors.

Eleven are the small islands around the treasure island.

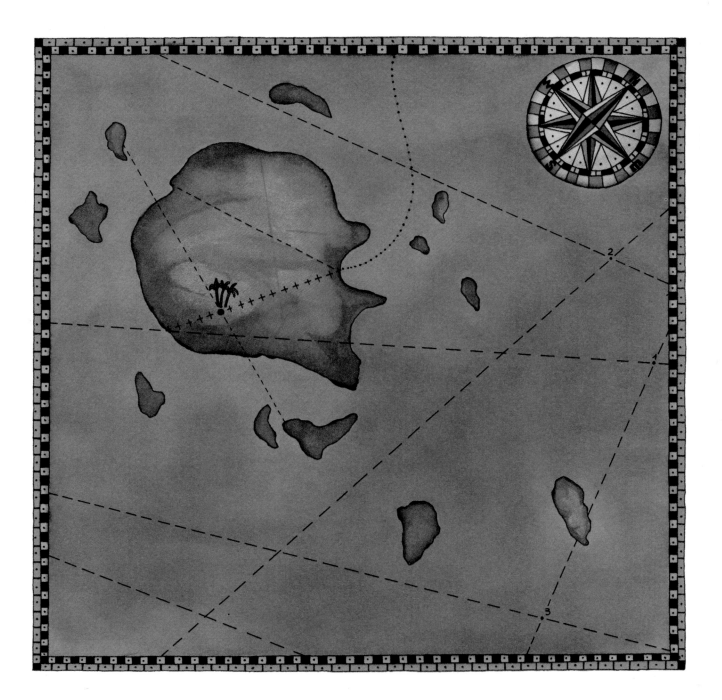

On the island are twelve treasure chests.
They are all empty except one.

You open it. There is a little treasure inside—
a pencil.

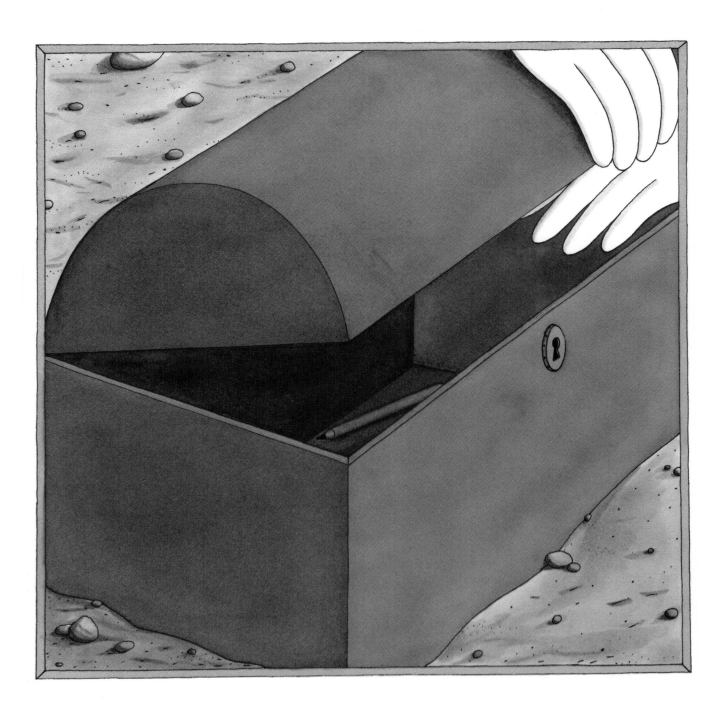